Ghulam Sarwar

Sex Education

The Muslim Perspective

FOURTH EDITION

THE MUSLIM EDUCATIONAL TRUST

1st Edition, September 1989
2nd Revised Edition, December 1992
3rd Revised Edition, October 1996
4th Edition, February 2004

British Library Cataloguing-in-Publication Data
A catalogue record of this book is available from the British Library

Published by:
The Muslim Educational Trust
130 Stroud Green Road
London N4 3RZ
UK
Tel: 020 7272 8502
Fax: 020 7281 3457
www.muslim-ed-trust-org.uk
email:info@muslim-ed-trust-org.uk

ISBN 0 907261 41 8

Printed and bound in Great Britain by:

The Cromwell Press Ltd.
Aintree Ave.
White Horse Business Park
Trowbridge, Wiltshire BA14 OXB
UK
Tel. 01225 711400

Contents

In the name of Allāh, The Most Merciful, The Most kind

Preface to the fourth edition

The third edition of my book *Sex Education – The Muslim Perspective* has sold out, by the blessings of Almighty *Allāh*. Since its first publication in 1989, there have been many legislative and other changes in the educational arena in England and Wales, the most significant of which in regard to sex education is the acceptance by the Government of the parental right of withdrawal from sex education lessons. The replacement of Circular 5/94 by Circular 0116/2000 by the (then) Department for Education and Employment (DFEE) has made significant changes in Sex and Relationships Education (SRE). Besides, the abolition of section 28 of the Local Government Act 1988 in 2003 and other legislative changes since 1996 have made a revision of the third edition a necessity.

I have made substantial additions and improvements to the text, making it an almost a new book. I am grateful to *Usāmah Ward, Dr. A. Jabbār Beg and Dr. Fārūq N. 'Ārefīn* for their comments and suggestions. I have benefited from the comments and suggestions made by: *Muḥammad Ibrāhīm* (formerly Ian Abrams), Head of RE (Religious Education) at Southgate School, Enfield; *Ruqaiyyah Waris Maqsood* (formerly Rosalyn Kendrick), former Head of RE at William Gee School, Hull; *Faṭma Diaa 'Amer*, former RE teacher at Whitefield School, London; and *Jameel Ṣiddīq*, former secondary school teacher and MET representative on Waltham Forest SACRE (Standing Advisory Councils on Religious Education). I thank them all, and pray to *Allāh* to reward them.

I hope, as with the first three editions, the book will continue to receive support from parents, teachers, pupils and all those concerned with education in the UK and abroad.

Finally, I implore Almighty *Allāh* to accept my humble efforts and grant me His pardon in the *Ākhirah* (life after death). *Āmīn.*

... And my success (in my task) can only come from Allāh.
In Him I trust and unto Him I turn.
{Al-Qur'ān, chapter 11, verse 88}

Dhul Ḥijjah 1424 AH
February 2004 CE

Ghulam Sarwar

Introduction

Education is the process by which children are prepared for life. It aims at the development of the total personality of a child. Islām encompasses every aspect of life and exhorts human beings to direct all their actions towards the attainment of *Allāh's* (God's) pleasure in order to lead a contented life in this world and in the Hereafter (the*Ākhirah*) :

Say: Truly, my prayer and my service of sacrifice,
my life and my death
are (all) for Allāh,
the Cherisher of the worlds...
{Al-Qur'ān, chapter 6, verse 162}

Our Lord! Give us good in this world
and good in the Hereafter,
and save us from the torment of the Fire.
{Al-Qur'ān, chapter 2, verse 201}

The pursuit of knowledge is an obligation on every Muslim, male and female, and this knowledge must prepare a person to be a worthy servant of Allāh who created human beings to worship and obey Him. He will judge them on the basis of their piety (*Taqwā*) – meticulous obedience to Allāh's commands.

I created the jinn and humankind
only that they should worship Me.
{Al-Qur'ān, chapter 51, verse 56}

... Surely, the most honourable among you in the sight of Allāh
is the one who is best in taqwā.
Lo! Allāh is Knower, Aware.
{Al-Qur'ān, chapter 49, verse 13}

"Seeking knowledge is obligatory for every Muslim (male and female)." {Ibn Mājah Ḥadīth 220. www.al-islam.com (Arabic)}

A Muslim should live by the tenets of Islām as *Allāh's* Vicegerent (*Khalīfah*) on the earth; all his actions should be guided by *Allāh's* commands as revealed in the Qur'ān and as demonstrated by the life example (*Sunnah*) of the Prophet Muḥammad ﷺ. It is within this framework that Muslim parents would like their children to be educated.

The Education Reform Act 1988 (ERA) states that children in maintained schools should be educated through a *balanced and broadly based curriculum* which

> *(a) Promotes the spiritual, moral, cultural, mental and physical development of pupils at the school and of society; and*
>
> *(b) Prepares such pupils for the opportunities, responsibilities and experiences of adult life*. [Sec. 1 (2)(a)(b)]

When education is regarded as a total concept it is obvious that sex education should be a part of it, since it is an important aspect of human life.

Section 46 of the Education (No 2) Act 1986 requires that:

> *"The local education authority by whom any county, voluntary or special school is maintained, and the governing body and head teacher of the school, shall take such steps as are reasonably practicable to secure that where sex education is given to any registered pupils at the school it is given* ***in such a manner as to encourage those pupils to have due regard to moral considerations and the value of family life****."* [our emphasis]

British Society is, to all intents and purposes, secular and materialistic in outlook, and matters such as "the spiritual and moral" aspects of life remain largely ignored or marginalised in terms of the actual curriculum applied in schools, contrary to the objective set in section 2 of the ERA. The efforts of the School Curriculum and Assessment Authority (SCAA), now called the Qualifications and Curriculum Authority (QCA), to restore spiritual and moral values are particularly welcome and commendable in this context.

Despite this, Muslim parents face problems with regard to sex education. Although they have to recognise that they cannot achieve an ideal solution to the educational problems faced by their children, it is possible to solve at least some of them by liaising and cooperating with other parents. A number of the concerns Muslims have towards educational matters are held in common with many non-muslims, e.g. improving the standard and quality of education; reducing the levels of truancy, violence, use of drugs and undisciplined behaviour in schools; and raising the standards of morality and decency. By coming together in cooperation with others, Muslim parents can avoid some of the undesirable and un-Islāmic things going on in schools today. In a democratic society it is possible for Muslim parents to air their views – within the framework of the law – and for these views to be given due consideration.

The main concern of Muslims is not whether there should be sex education in schools. The need for sex education is not in question, especially when permissiveness and liberalised social attitudes have led to early sexual experimentation resulting in increasing number of abortions, school-age mothers and fathers, family stress, children born to unmarried couples and one-parent families. Rather, Muslims feel that the methodology and content used to teach this sensitive subject often contravene Islāmic values of decency, modesty and responsibility, and the debate centres on where, how and by whom sex education is to be given. The fact that sex education is a part of the School Curriculum and of the National Science Curriculum, the onus is on schools to provide such education. Muslims would need to be reassured that the principles of Islām are given due consideration by schools and others responsible for such education and are not being violated in any way. Indeed, Islāmic values would provide a firm and balanced foundation for any sex education programme.

Allāh,The Creator, says in His final book of revealed guidance, the Qur'ān:

> ***Does man think that he will be left uncontrolled,***
> ***(without purpose)?***
> ***Was he not a drop of sperm emitted (in lowly form)?***
> ***Then did he become a leech-like clot*** [***'alaqah***]***;***
> ***then did (Allāh) make and fashion (him) in due proportion.***
> ***{Al-Qur'ān, chapter 75, verses 36–38}***
>
> ***Man We did create from a quintessence (of clay).***
> ***Then We placed him as (a drop of) sperm in a place of rest,***
> ***firmly fixed.***
> ***Then We made the sperm into a leech-like clot*** [***'alaqah***]***;***
> ***then of that clot We made a (foetus) lump;***

then we made out of that lump bones
and clothed the bones with flesh;
then we developed out of it another creature.
So blessed be Allāh, the Best of Creators!
{Al-Qur'ān, chapter 23, verses 12–14}

So let man see from what he is created!
He is created from a drop emitted,
proceeding from between the backbone and the ribs.
{Al-Qur'ān, chapter 86, verses 5–7}

They question you (O Muḥammad) concerning menstruation.
Say, it is an illness, so keep away from women during menses.
and do not approach them until they are cleansed,
when they have purified themselves,
then go in unto them as Allāh has enjoined upon you.
Allāh loves those who turn to Him in repentance
and loves those who purify themselves.
{Al-Qur'ān, chapter 2, verse 222}

The above verses clearly mention the process of procreation. These verses together with the many sayings of Prophet Muḥammad ﷺ should provide a firm basis for any sex education programme.

"... Whoever among you can marry, should marry, because it helps him lower his gaze and guard his modesty..."
{Al-Bukhārī, Volume 7, Book 62, Number 4, Page 4}

"...and in your sexual relations there is Ṣadaqah [charity]..."
{Muslim Vol. 2, Ḥadīth 2198, p. 482}

Family life, with marriage at the core and care for both children and parents as its basic tenet, is strongly recommended in Islām. Sex education must be looked at with this concept firmly in mind. Without such a holistic outlook it is almost impossible to understand Islāmic teachings fully. Every aspect of human life has a common purpose in Islām; human sexuality is no exception.

[References from the collections of the Prophet's sayings (Aḥādīth, plural of Ḥadīth) have been taken from: Ṣaḥīḥ Al-Bukhārī, Ṣaḥīḥ Muslim, Sunan Abū Dāwūd, Sunan Ibn Mājah, Jāmi' At-Tirmidhī, Sunan An-Nasā'ī, Al-Muwaṭṭa of Imām Mālik and Sunan Ad-Dailamī.]

The Islāmic attitude to sexual relationships

Islām gives practical and beneficial guidance for all aspects of life, including human sexuality. Allāh, the Creator likes ease and comfort for mankind.

> ***Allah intends ease for you; and He does not intend (to make things) difficult for you.***
> ***{Al-Qur'ān, chapter 2, verse 185}***

In Islām, marriage is considered the only channel for fulfilling sexual urges. Sexual relationships outside marriage are totally forbidden and incur severe penalties in this life and in the Hereafter. Islām emphasizes the prevention of social crimes rather than the proliferation of opportunities for them and Islāmic law prescribes severe punishments for sex-related offences (adultery, fornication, homosexuality, rape, etc.) which are regarded as both anti-social and anti-family.

> ***The woman and the man guilty of adultery or fornication,***
> ***flog each of them with a hundred stripes.***
> ***Let not compassion move you in their case,***
> ***in a matter prescribed by Allāh,***
> ***if you believe in Allāh and the Last Day.***
> ***And let a party of the believers witness the punishment.***
> ***{Al-Qur'ān, chapter 24, verse 2}***

> ***And approach not fornication or adultery;***
> ***surely it is shameful and an evil way.***
> ***{Al-Qur'ān, chapter 17, verse 32}***

The Islāmic penal code emphasizes the stability and security of family and social life at the expense, if necessary, of unlimited individual freedom. It is based on divine guidance and wisdom, and is the best way of creating a safe and secure society.

Cleanliness (*Ṭahārah*), which has been equated by Prophet Muḥammad ﷺ to half of the faith {Muslim Vol. 1, No. 432, p. 147}, is one of the basic tenets of Islām. The *Qur'ān* prescribes a bath (*Ghusl*) after menstruation, post-childbirth bleeding, wet dreams and intimate sexual contact.

The *Qur'ān* also states that the sexual relationship has the aim not only of procreation, but also of physical enjoyment and achieving peace of mind; husband and wife are described as being 'garments' for each other, each to provide love, mercy, warmth and comfort for one another.

It is made lawful to you, on the night of the fasts,
to have sexual relations with your wives.
They are your garments and you are their garments...
So, now have sexual relations with them,
and seek what Allāh has ordained for you...
{Al-Qur'ān, chapter 2, verse 187}

Arranging a marriage in Islām

In Islām, marriage is the basis of the family which, in turn, is the basis for a stable society. Marriage itself is a legally binding contract between a man and a woman which establishes their intention and mutual commitment to live together according to the teachings of their faith. They must remember their duty to *Allāh* and to each other at all times, and that they have rights and responsibilities over one another.

O mankind, be dutiful to Your Lord (Creator)
Who created you from a single person, (Ādam)
And from him created his wife,
and from them both He created
many men and women;
Fear Allāh, through whom you demand your mutual (rights)
and (do not cut the relations of) the wombs (kinship):
Surely, Allāh ever watches over you.
{Al-Qur'ān, chapter 4, verse 1}

Prohibited to you (for marriage) are:
your mothers, daughters, sisters;
your father's sisters, your mother's sisters,
your brother's daughters, your sister's daughters;

your foster-mothers (who suckled you), your foster-sisters;
your wives' mothers;
your step-daughters under your guardianship,
born of your wives to whom you have gone in
– but there is no sin if you have not gone in them –
the wives of your sons
who (spring) from your loins;
and two sisters in wedlock at one and the same time...
{Al-Qur'ān, chapter 4, verse 23}

The method by which some Muslims select marriage partners is often regarded as old-fashioned by non-Muslims. As Islām emphasizes chastity and modesty, there is normally no unnecessary social contact between young Muslim men and women, especially of the kind which is regarded as perfectly normal in a non-Muslim society. There is no such thing as dating or premarital intimacy of any kind in Islām. Sexual behaviour and acts are only for those who are legally within the security of a marriage. There should be no sexual experimentation before marriage and fidelity within marriage is essential.

Islam gives young people the right to express their preference and say what they are looking for in a prospective partner. However, it is not the usual practice for them actively to seek a partner for themselves, although if done within Islamic guidelines this is not blameworthy. Such seeking is mostly done by their parents, or other elders within the family. In other words, it is usually an 'arranged marriage'. It is important to note that such arranged marriages *must meet the basic condition of the freely given consent of both the bride and the groom.* A *forced* marriage, where consent has not been given by either the bride or groom, or is given only under excessive pressure, is contrary to the teachings of Islām. Such marriages are to be treated as having no legal basis in Islām. Some Muslim parents do place undue pressure on their children, especially their daughters, in the choice of partner for marriage; in particular, they may place greater emphasis on 'family honour' than on the welfare and happiness of their children. Such behaviour may have horrific consequences, For example, "Honour killings" although rare are used as a propoganda tool against Islām, and are given extensive coverage in the media. Islām never condones such horrible and nonsensical conduct. Forced marriages are unislāmic. Open and frank discussion about marriage between parents and their children could help avoid misunderstandings and unreasonable exercise of parental authority.

Arranged marriages, then, are the general custom amongst Muslims as the best way to find, vet and meet potential husbands or wives within the overall context of the Islāmic way of life. Once a potential match is arranged, the most important Islāmic requirement is the freely given consent of both the prospective bride and groom; without this, the marriage should not proceed. Arranged marriages are not, of course, unique to Muslims; other religious and cultural groups use similar matchmaking methods and such marriages are generally more stable and are less likely to end in divorce than marriages based on pre-marital emotional and sexual experimentation or experience. It must be noted that in Islām marriage is a simple matter and an adult Muslim male and female are free to enter into a marriage contract in the presence of two witnesses. An arranged marriage is a useful and convenient system. The new Muslims in the west would have to seek out their partners in life within the limits of Islām. Friends and Imāms could act as their representatives to choose their partners in life.

Prophet Muḥammad ﷺ has given clear guidance on the qualities to look for in a potential partner in marriage:

> *"A woman is married for four things: her wealth, her family status, her beauty and her religion. So you should marry the religious woman (otherwise) you will be a loser."*
> *{Al-Bukhārī Vol. 7, Ḥadīth 27, pp. 18 –19 & Muslim Vol. 2, Hadīth 3457, p. 749}*

> *"Do not marry only for the sake of beauty, as perhaps the beauty will become the cause of moral decline. Do not marry even for the sake of wealth, as perhaps the wealth will become the reason for disobedience. Marry rather on the grounds of religious devotion."*
> *{Ibn Mājah, Ḥadīth 1849. www.al-islam.com}*

Another essential condition of a Muslim marriage agreement is payment of the *mahr* (dowry or marital gift). This has to be paid by the man to the woman (not the reverse as in some cultures) and is for the use of the woman alone unless she decides otherwise. It may take the form of cash, jewellery or even teaching the bride a part of the *Qur'ān*. Payment of *mahr* is a condition of an

Islāmic marriage and it should be both affordable by the bridegroom and consistent with the social position of the bride; she may, if she wishes, forgo all or part of it after the marriage at her pleasure, but she must not be forced to forgo it. The concept of *mahr* is at the heart of the economic freedom of women in Islām. The amount of the *mahr* should not act as a deterrent to the prospective husband. Those who do not have the means to marry should practice regular fasting and seek *Allāh's* help to enable them to get married.

> ***But let those who find not (financial means for) marriage keep themselves chaste (from sexual relations) until Allāh enriches them of His Bounty.***
> ***{Al-Qur'ān, chapter 24, verse 33}***

> *"O young people! Whoever among you can marry, should marry, because it helps him lower his gaze and guard his modesty (i.e. his private parts from committing illegal sexual intercourse, etc.) and whoever is not able to marry, should fast, as fasting diminishes his sexual desire."*
> *{Al-Bukhārī Vol. 7, Ḥadīth 4, p. 4 & Muslim Vol. 2, Ḥadīth 3231 pp. 702–703}*

The roles of husband and wife

Islām recognises that there are physical and mental differences between men and women. Husbands and wives are companions for each other, and they have clearly defined roles within the family. The husband is responsible for the economic maintenance of the family, and the wife is responsible for the management of the household affairs.The family responsibilities are shared between them.

> ***Men are the supporters of women...***
> ***{Al-Qur'ān, chapter 4, verse 34}***

> ***... And they (women) have rights (in over their husband as regards their living expenses) as similar (to those of their husbands) over them (as regards obedience and respect etc.) to what is reasonable, but men have a degree (of responsibility over them) ... {Al-Qur'ān, chapter 2, verse 228}***

Even if her wealth is greater than her husband's, she is under no obligation to support the family financially, although, of course, she may if she wishes. She should obey her husband at all times unless he specifically asks her to disobey *Allāh*. Husbands must be considerate towards their wives and concerned for their welfare. At all times, both husband and wife must reserve their sexuality exclusively for each other.

A Muslim woman, married or single, is a person in her own right; she is not merely an adjunct to her husband, father or brothers. Islāmic law preceded modern Western law by thirteen centuries in granting women the right to own property and have their own earnings (even after marriage), something she may or may not share with her husband; the decision is hers. The stereotype image of Muslim women as servants forever in the house cooking and cleaning, with no spirituality, personality, interests or personal life, has no basis in Islāmic teachings. Men and women are completely equal in terms of accountability to *Allāh*. However, equal doesn't mean 'the same' – physical differences and capabilities alone should demonstrate that – but both have the same religious obligations and, if *Allāh* wills it, the same rewards in this life and in the Hereafter.

It is common for critics of Islām to try to 'prove' that Islām does not treat men and women equally by quoting the inheritance laws, by which men inherit a bigger share of an estate than women. But if we consider the point mentioned earlier about the responsibility men have of looking after the women in their household, it should be clear that a larger inheritance helps to defray such an additional financial burden. What the women don't get as a direct legacy, they get indirectly through the inheritance of the male responsible for their upkeep.

There are many Qur'ānic verses and sayings of Prophet Muḥammad ﷺ that entreat men to show kindness and consideration for women. Muslim men should always show great respect, honour and tenderness to their wives.

> ***Treat them (wives) politely; even if you dislike them, perhaps you dislike (in them) something in which Allāh has placed much good. {Al-Qur'an, chapter 4, verse 19}***

Both men and women have freedom to contribute to society in keeping with their own particular skills and interests, providing they maintain their personal dignity and modesty, and keep within the limits set by Islām. Women can fulfil many essential roles in society (e.g. in education, medicine and social work); at the time of the Prophet ﷺ women were active in the struggle against paganism. Prophet Muḥammad's ﷺ wives (may *Allāh* be pleased with them) were consulted by many people (men and women); among them, 'Ā'ishah was an expert on the sayings of the Prophet ﷺ and Islāmic jurisprudence. She was also considered amongst the foremost companions (of Prophet Muḥammad ﷺ), being part of a select group whose opinion on legal issues (Fatāwā) was considered binding.

The tone for the marriage relationship is set by *Allāh* in the *Qur'ān*:

> ***And among His signs is this,***
> ***that He created for you mates from among yourselves,***
> ***that you may dwell in tranquillity with them***
> ***and He has put love and mercy between your hearts:***
> ***verily in that are signs for those who reflect.***
> ***{Al-Qur'ān, chapter 30, verse 21}***

Thus, there should be mutual respect, kindness, love, companionship and harmonious interaction between husband and wife. Although, in practice, women generally do the domestic work in a Muslim home, this is not a legal requirement. Differences based on allocated areas of responsibilities are intended to be complementary and not competitive. Primarily, men are bread winners and women are homemakers.

> *"Surely! Everyone of you is a guardian and is responsible for his charges: the Imām (ruler) of the people is a guardian and is responsible for his subjects; a man is a guardian of his family (household) and is responsible for his subjects; a woman is the guardian of her husband's home and of his children and is responsible for them; and the slave of a man is a guardian of his master's property and is responsible for it. Surely, everyone of you is a guardian and is responsible for his charges."*
>
> *{Al-Bukhārī, Volume 9, Ḥadīth 252, p.190}*

Men should, however, help their wives in household chores, following the example of the Prophet ﷺ who helped his wives with domestic chores regularly, mended his own clothes and milked the goats.

In a Muslim marriage, both husband and wife have a responsibility to meet one another's sexual needs. There should be no extramarital sexual activity for married Muslims (nor, as stated earlier, premarital intimacy for unmarried Muslims). Adultery and fornication are not only serious sins but also – in Islāmic law – serious crimes with severe punishments. The reason is obvious when you look at the disruption to family life and society in general as a result of adulterous behaviour.

Any act that destabilises marriage will also destabilise society. Hence, the Islāmic punishments for such acts are severe and are intended to act as a deterrent in order to develop a stable and healthy moral society. The punishments for fornication and adultery (*Zinā*) fall within prescribed limits (*Ḥudūd*, sing. *Ḥadd*), they have stringent conditions, often involving the need for witnesses with non-contradictory statements. Such punishments in the history of Islām are few yet they have successfully served their purpose of deterrance. They cannot be applied in an anarchic sense and can only be enforced in an Islāmic society implementing Sharī'āh (Islāmic Law) in its totality. This is only possible in a fully-fledged Islāmic state.

The punishment for fornication and sodomy is one hundred lashes. Married men and women found guilty of adultery are to be stoned to death. A rapist incurs the same punishment as a married adulterer. Prophet Muḥammad ﷺ said:

> *When an unmarried male commits fornication with an unmarried female, they should receive one hundred lashes and exile for one year. And in the case of a married male committing adultery with a married female, they shall receive one hundred lashes and be stoned to death.*
> *{Muslim Vol. 3, Ḥadīth No. 4191, p. 911}*

The punishment for someone who falsely accuses another of fornication or adultery (*Qadhf*), is eighty lashes and the permanent ineligibility of being a witness in a court of law.

> ***And those who launch a charge against chaste women,***
> ***and produce not four wittnesses (to support their allegations),***
> ***flog them with eighty stripes;***
> ***and reject their evidence ever after:***

for such men are wicked transgressors.
Unless they repent thereafter and mend (their conduct);
for Allāh is Oft-forgiving, Most Merciful.
And for those who launch a charge against their spouses,
and have (in support) no evidence but their own,
their solitary evidence (can be received)
if they bear witness four times (with an oath) by Allāh
that they are solemnly telling the truth;
and the fifth (oath) (should be) that they solemnly invoke the curse of Allāh on themselves
if they tell a lie.
But it would avert the punishment from the wife,
if she bears witness four times (with an oath) by Allāh,
that (her husband) is telling a lie;
and the fifth (oath) should be
that she solemnly invokes the wrath of Allāh on herself
if (her accuser) is telling the truth.
If it were not for Allāh's grace and mercy on you,
and that Allāh is Oft-Returning, full of Wisdom,
(you would be ruined indeed.)
{Al-Qur'ān, chapter 24, verses 4–10}

The Prophet ﷺ mentioned the slandering of chaste women as one of seven deadly sins that Muslims should stay away from.

Narrated Abū Hurairah: The Prophet ﷺ said , "Avoid the seven great destructive sins." The people enquired, " O Allāh's Messenger! What are they?" He said, "To join others in worship along with Allāh, sorcery, killing a person whose killing Allāh prohibited except justly, eating up ribā (usury), eating up an orphan's wealth, giving back to the enemy and fleeing from the battlefield at the time of fighting, and falsely accusing chaste believing women, of illegal sexual intercourse."
{Al-Bukhārī, Vol. 4, Ḥadīth 28, p.23}

The Prophet ﷺ discouraged anything that might lead to promiscuity, saying:

The Zinā of the eye is the lustful look;
and the Zinā of the ears is listening to voluptuous music and singing
and the Zinā of the tongue is licentious speech;
and the Zinā of the hand is the lustful grip (embrace)
and the Zinā of the feet is to walk to (to the place) where he intends to commit adultery, walking towards the desires.
{Muslim Vol. 4 Ḥadīth 6422 p.1398}

It is interesting to note *Biblical* sayings on this subject:

You shall not commit adultery.
{Exodus 20:14}

When a man is discovered lying with a married woman,
they shall both die,
the woman as well as the man who lay with her,
you shall rid Israel of this wickedness.

When a virgin is pledged in marriage to a man
and another man comes upon her in the town and lies with her,
you shall bring both of them out to the gate of that town
and stone both of them to death;
the girl because, although in the town, she did not cry for help,
and the man because he dishonoured another man's wife;
you shall rid yourselves of this wickedness.
{Deuteronomy 22:22 – 24}

Do not commit adultery…
{Matthew 19:18, Mark 10:19, Luke 18:20}

Divorce

Unlike many marriages in the West, where premarital love and intimacy are increasingly common, the basic ingredient for a successful Muslim marriage is a shared set of values upon which to build a life together. A shared belief in *Islām* can often bind couples together in their relationship allowing them to withstand many of the pressures exerted by contemporary Western societies which eventually force many couples apart. Prophet Muḥammad ﷺ said:

> *"Of all things which have been permitted, divorce is the most hated by Allāh."*
> *{Abū Dāwūd, Ḥadīth. 2173. The Hadith Software Version 1.0 }*

A Muslim marriage is seen as a real relationship between two individuals who cannot, realistically, be expected to be 100% immune from the stress and strain of everyday life. Islām's emphasis is on the continuation of a marriage which ensures happiness, love, warmth and contentment, and the welfare of children. Their shared faith will help to cushion a Muslim couple from the worst effects of marital problems. Nevertheless, Islām is realistic enough to prepare couples for the possibility that they might not be able to carry on together as husband and wife, for a variety of reasons, and so divorce – although disliked – is allowed when all conciliatory efforts have failed. It is essential that a marriage should be harmonious and not injurious to the life and health of the couple and their families and, ultimately, society at large.

In 2002, the number of divorces granted in the UK increased by 1.9 per cent, from 157,000 in 2001 to 160,000. There is an increasing trend within the UK and across most of Europe of falling marriage rates and marital breakdown. (See: Office for National Statistics, UK, www.statistics.gov.uk). Such an increase could be due to an increasingly relaxed attitude towards marriage and what sort of commitment it entails. This results in divorces on the slightest grounds, namely 'behavioural issues'. This type of attitude is against Islāmic teachings which encourage patience to sustain a marriage.

The other extreme can be seen in some cultures where divorce is totally prohibited, often resulting in drastic consequence: "Indian Government statistics show that husbands and in-laws killed nearly 7,000 women in 2001 over inadequate dowry payments." (See: 'India's dowry deaths', http://news.bbc.co.uk/1/hi/programmes/crossing_continents/3071963.stm , as updated till

16 July, 2003) . In many cases such deaths could have been avoided except for the stigma attached to divorce compelling the bride to live intolerable conditions eventually resulting in her death.

Islam shows the middle path: it permits divorce, as sometimes it is the only solution to serious problems of marital discord, yet it discourages a flippant relaxed attitude that advcoates divorce on any pretext whatsoever. A husband who dislikes a certain trait in his wife might discover that she possesses other qualities that appeal to him.

The Qur'ān provides general guidelines for the process of divorce upholding the values of justice, fairness and kindness . (Al- Qur'ān, chapter 2: 227–237, chapter 65:1–12)

The regulations of Islam on family life, matrimony, and the respective positions of men and women, serve as a model which all nations would do well to emulate.

Sexual etiquette of Islām

This book is not intended to be a detailed guide on marital relationships in Islām. However, the following points may be regarded as the parameters within which marital sexual relationships should be conducted.

- All sexual encounters in Islām must be within a marriage, which is a solemn binding contract entered into voluntarily by a man and a woman in the name of *Allāh*. Islām allows no extramarital relationships.
- The husband and wife are vicegerents (*Khulafā'*) of *Allāh* on the Earth. They are expected to obey the commands of their Creator as contained in the *Qur'ān* and the example (*Sunnah*) of Prophet Muḥammad ﷺ.
- The purposes of sexual intercourse within marriage are: procreation; physical pleasure and contentment; love, warmth and kindness between husband and wife; and building a stable, happy, coherent and purposeful society for the pleasure of *Allāh*.

The sexual act between husband and wife is also rewarded in the Afterlife (Ākhirah), as Prophet Muḥammad ﷺ said:

"... and in man's sexual intercourse (with his wife) there is a Ṣadaqah (charity)." They (the companions) said, "O Messenger of Allāh, is there reward for him who satisfies his sexual passion among us?" He ﷺ said, "Tell me, if he were to devote it to something forbidden, would it not be a sin on his part? Similarly, if he were to devote it to something lawful, he should have a reward."
{Muslim Vol. 2 Ḥadīth 2198, p. 482}

- Sexual intercourse should begin with a prayer *(Du'ā')* by the husband and *wife:*

  'In the name of Allāh, O Allāh! protect me from Satan and protect what you bestow upon us [*i.e. a child*] *from Satan.' The Prophet î said, "After that, if Allāh decrees that they will have a child, Satan will never be able to harm that child."*
  {Al-Bukhārī Vol. 7 Ḥadīth 094, p. 70}

- All sexual activities between husband and wife must be within the context of natural modesty (*Ḥayā'*), warmth, kindness, decency, family life and morality. Neither of them should do anything unwholesome and distasteful.

- Sexual relations between husband and wife must take place in private and neither party should divulge their sex-related secrets to anyone. Prophet Muḥammad ﷺ is reported to have said that the disclosure of sex-related secrets by either a husband or his wife is:

  "like a female Satan who meets a male Satan on the roadside and has intercourse in full public view."
  {Abū Dāwūd Ḥadīth 2169. The Hadith Software Version 1.0}

- A husband and wife may choose any convenient, enjoyable and satisfying position and method for sexual intercourse, with the exception of anal intercourse, which is prohibited and severely condemned. The Prophet ﷺ said:

  "He who has intercourse with his wife through her anus is accursed."
  {Abū Dāwūd Ḥadīth 2157. The Hadith Software Version 1.0}

- Foreplay is strongly encouraged, the sexual act should not be reduced to the simple satisfaction of an animalistic instinct – rather it should be the fostering of intimacy between the partners which increases with time.

"No one of you should fall upon his wife like an animal; rather, let there first be a messenger between you." "And what is that messenger?" they asked, and he ﷺ replied, "kisses and words." *{Ad-Dailamī}*

- Intercourse during menstruation and post-childbirth bleeding is not allowed. All other sexual activities – such as kissing and touching, etc. – are allowed at these times. Menstruation is a biological phenomenon created by Allāh, and it should not be regarded as making women unclean. They carry on with their normal routine in life with the exception of some religious duties and sexual intercourse.

- A man should treat his wife with kindness and tenderness. Husbands should be particularly considerate when wives are suffering from menstruation and other illnesses. Prophet Muḥammad ﷺ said:

  "The best of you all are those who are best to their wives."
  {Mishkātul-Maṣābīḥ Ḥadīth 3264, MacHadith}

- A bath *(Ghusl)* is obligatory when in *janābah*, i.e. after sexual intercourse, wet dreams, menstruation and post-childbirth bleeding. Without this one should not offer the obligatory prayers.

  ... And if you are in state of janābah, purify yourselves ...
  {Al-Qur'ān, chapter 5, verse 6}

  O you who believe!
  Do not offer your prayer... when you are Junub
  except when you are travelling on the road
  till you have taken a bath...
  {Al-Qur'ān, chapter 4, verse 43}

  It is reported that the Prophet ﷺ said:

  "When the circumcised part touches the circumcised part, a bath (ghusl) is compulsory."
  {Muwaṭṭā of Mālik Ḥadīth 75. The Hadith Software Version 1.0}

Between acts of sexual intercourse, or before sleeping after intercourse, it is recommended to wash the private parts and perform ablution *(wuḍū')* as if for prayer. One of his companions, 'Umar, told the Prophet ﷺ:

"I became Junub at night," and he was told, "Perform ablution, after washing your private parts, and then sleep."
{Al-Bukhārī Vol. 1, Ḥadīth 288, p. 174}

In addition, when he was asked:

"May any one of us sleep whilst in Janaba?" the Prophet replied, "Yes, if you perform ablution."
{Al-Bukhārī Vol. 1, Ḥadīth 287, p. 174}

This shows that *Ghusl* does not have to be done straight away; but it must be done before the next prayer.

It is clearly good manners to be clean before sexual activity also.

- A wife should not refuse to have sexual intercourse with her husband without a reasonable excuse, as the Prophet ﷺ said:

"If a husband invites his wife to his bed (i.e. to have sexual relation) and she refuses and causes him to sleep in anger, the angels curse her till the morning."
{Al-Bukhārī Vol. 4, Ḥadīth 460, p. 302}

Similarly, a husband should not ignore the sexual needs of his wife.

- The majority of scholars of Islām do not allow masturbation. This opinion is based on the following verse:

Those who guard their sexual organs
except with their spouses
or those whom their right hands possess
for (with regard to them) they are without blame.
But those who crave something beyond that are transgressors.
{Al-Qur'ān, chapter 23, verses 5–7}

Imām Aḥmad bin Ḥanbal (d. 855 CE) and Ibn Ḥazm (d. 1064 CE) permitted it in only two circumstances: when there is a fear of committing fornication; and if there is a financial inability to marry (page 170. The Lawful and the

Prohibited in Islām by Yusuf Al-Qaradawi ATP, USA) . However, the Prophet ﷺ gave this advice to control sexual urges:

"O young people! Whoever among you can marry, should marry, because it helps him lower his gaze and guard his modesty (i.e. his private parts from committing illegal sexual intercourse, etc.) and whoever is not able to marry, should fast, as fasting diminishes his sexual desire."
{Al-Bukhārī Vol. 7, Ḥadīth 4, p. 4}

- Bondage, whipping, sado-masochism, and other depraved means of achieving sexual satisfaction contradict starkly with the very purpose of sexual relationships.
- Dress that is likely to arouse sexual passions is allowed only in the exclusive presence of the marital partner.
- When going out among people with whom marriage is possible (*Ghair Maḥram* – according to Islāmic law), women should wear modest dress *(Hijāb)*, covering the whole body (except the face and hands) in such a way and with such material that does not show the contours of the body, either by being too tight or by being transparent.

Tell the believing men to lower their gaze
and guard their private parts.
That is purer for them. Surely Allāh knows what they do.
And tell the believing women to lower their gaze
and guard their private parts
and not to display their beauty except what is apparent,
to draw their cloaks over their bosom
and not to reveal their adornment
except to their husbands or fathers or their husband's father
or their sons or their husband's sons
or their brothers or their brothers' sons
or their sisters' sons or their women or their maids
or impotent male servants
or children who do not know of women's private parts.
And let them not walk noisily
so as to reveal what they preserve of their beauty.

And all of you beg Allāh to forgive you, O believers
in order that you may be successful.
{Al-Qur'ān, chapter 24, verses 30–31}

- *'Awrah* refers to those parts of the body which modesty requires to be covered. For males, the *'awrah* is that part of the body between the navel and the knees; for females, it is the whole body except the face and hands. A man is not allowed to bare his *'awrah* before anyone except his wife and *vice versa*. In addition, a woman should not show any part of her body from the chest to the knees even to males whom she cannot marry (e.g. her father, brother, son, uncle, nephew, etc.). In other words, she can go without a headcovering or with a sleeveless garment, for example, in front of these men if she wishes. Further, she should not show any part of her body between the navel and the knees to a Muslim female, nor any part of her *'awrah* at all to any non-Muslim female.
- Pornography is forbidden in Islām, as it entails numerous violations of Islāmic laws, such as those relating to modesty of dress, privacy in sexual matters, and has detrimental effects on both society and the individual.

Homosexuality

Section 28 of the Local Government Act 1988 prohibits local authorities from intentionally promoting homosexuality or publishing material with that intention and from promoting the teaching in any maintained school of the acceptability of homosexuality. This Section has been repealed in 2003, because of the pressure created by gay lobbies, with slogans such as "coming out of the closet" and "sexual liberty and freedom". Pressure formed by these lobbies on political and legal institutions, the media, and society in general has resulted in a radically different definition and concept of homosexuality in the mindset of the common person in Britain. **Recent legislation proposals contained in the Queen's speech given on 27 November 2003, allowing for the registration of civil partnerships between same-sex couples went almost unnoticed amidst a furore about escalating university tuition fees.** Equally shocking was the recent consecration of the first openly gay Bishop within the Anglican church in the United States (See: Profile of Gene Robinson, The Guardian, October 31 2003). Such legislative proposals sound the death knell for marriage and family life, having catastrophic social, economical and moral consequences.

Up until 1970 the British psychiatric establishment broadly classified homosexuality as a 'mental disorder'. In 1973 the Nomenclature Committee of the *Diagnostic and Statistical Manual of Mental Disorders (DSM),* the official reference book for diagnosing mental disorders in America and throughout much of the world, responding to pressure from homosexual activist groups, voted for the elimination of 'homosexuality' from it's official diagnostic categories of mental illness. (See: "An Instant Cure", *Time* magazine, 1 April,1974, p. 45)

Islām like most other major faiths of the world, categorically forbids homosexual practices (sexual relations between two men or between two women), regarding them as a great sin. In a society under Islāmic law, such would be severely punished.

Of all the creatures in the world,
will you approach males,
and leave those whom Allāh has created for you to be your mates?
Indeed, you are a people transgressing (all limits).
{Al-Qur'an, 26: 165–166}

And (remember) Lot when he said to his people:
"Do you commit indecency (great sin, sodomy etc.) with your eyes open?
Do you approach men lustfully instead of women?
No, you are a people who behave senselessly."
{Al-Qur'an, 27: 54–55}

Prophet Muḥammad ﷺ said: *"If you find anyone doing as Lot's people did (i.e. homosexual sodomy), kill the one who does it, and the one to whom it is done."*
{Abū Dāwūd, Ḥadīth 4447. The Hadith Software Version 1.0}

These verses refer to the society of Lot (Lūṭ, peace be upon him). Allāh sent Lot to warn his people of the evil of their ways. They ignored these warnings. Eventually Allāh commanded Lot to leave with his family, whereafter He destroyed the whole town and all its inhabitants, because of their homosexual practices. Muslim jurists have held differing opinions concerning the punishment for this abominable practice, some stating the punishment for fornication, while some stating the death penalty for both the active and passive participants. It is important to mention that these rulings are not given in an anarchic sense where a Muslim takes the law into his own hands. Rather for these punishments to be implemented, due legal process needs to be carried out, which can only be done under a state implementing Islamic Law. While such punishments may seem cruel, they have been suggested to maintain the purity of the society and to keep it clean of perverted elements, allowing for the spiritual development of its members in an ideal environment. The spread of this depraved practice in a society disrupts its natural life pattern and makes those who practice it slaves to their lusts, depriving them of decent taste, decent morals, and a decent manner of living.

The institution of family is crucially important in Islām, and the rules governing interaction between the sexes are there to prevent harmful acts such as fornication and adultery. As we have said, outside of the immediate family, men and women must dress modestly, according to Islāmic guidelines. Free mixing is strongly discouraged, this all helps to prevent forbidden relationships.

Homosexuality presents a problem. It is not suggested that men will not mix with each other, nor that women will not mix with each other; they can do so within the limits set by the *Qur' ān* and the *Sunnah* of Prophet Muḥammad ﷺ. Those who seek to fulfil homosexual desires necessarily damage the very fabric of society which is why Islām condemns such practices.

It is worth commenting on the terms **'homophobia'** and **'heterosexism'**. Homophobia generally means a fear of homosexuals or homosexuality. The Islāmic viewpoint is not homophobic; disapproval is different from fear. Heterosexism has been defined as heterosexuals believing they are superior which justifies imposing values. In Islām it is not a question of superiority or inferiority, but one of right or wrong, in the same way that Islām says that theft is wrong or that murder is wrong.

Whilst Islām forbids homosexual practices, it does not seek out those with homosexual desires with a view to persecuting them. If people have such desires, they should keep them to themselves, and should control their desires to avoid forbidden practices. The advice would be the same as, say, to someone who had sexual desires for minors or for close family: that having the desires does not legitimise realising them. Islām aims at closing all avenues that might encourage evil practice which could corrupt and pollute the whole society.

Promiscuity, sexually transmitted diseases and AIDS

Promiscuity, both heterosexual and homosexual, leads to innumerable problems: for an Islāmic society, based as it is on family life, trust, fidelity, love and accountability to *Allāh*, promiscuous behaviour based solely on selfish physical gratification with little care for the ultimate consequences of one's actions is totally unacceptable. Apart from the break-ups of family relationships (with the resultant proliferation of single-parent families and the psychological effects on adults and children alike) such behaviour spreads both physical and mental diseases, a case in point being AIDS.

Of course, a cure must be found (*Allāh* willing) to help those unfortunate enough to be HIV positive (which may lead to 'full-blown' AIDS). Such efforts are a humanitarian necessity. However, while the medical scientists are trying to make a breakthrough in their search for a cure, Islām has some very positive and radical things to say about how the disease is caught and spread in the first place.

> Prophet Muḥammad ﷺ said, *"Every intoxicant is khamr and every khamr is Ḥarām [forbidden]."*
> *{Muslim Vol. 3, Ḥadīth 4963, 4964 & 4966 p.1108}*

> Prophet Muḥammad ﷺ said, *"If fornication should become widespread, you should realise that this has never happened without new diseases befalling the people which their forebears never suffered."*
> *{Ibn Mājah, Ḥadīth 4009. www.al-islam.com (Arabic)}*

> ***Let those who find not the wherewithal for marriage keep themselves chaste until Allāh gives them the means out of His grace.***
> ***{Al-Qur'ān, chapter 24, verse 33}***

HIV is mostly transmitted as a result of drug abuse, sexual promiscuity and homosexual acts, all forbidden in Islām. However, these days anyone who declares that homosexuality is a perverted way of life – as Muslims must – is accused of intolerance. Muslims believe, though, that such behaviour has been forbidden by *Allāh* (God) for very real reasons and if we ignore His guidance there are bound to be harmful effects on society. Tragically, HIV has now spread to the innocent through unfaithful husbands and wives, infected blood transfusions, as well as to children born to infected parents. If people had all followed the way of life of Islām, no one would have suffered and died from AIDS. By the end of 2003, 37 million adults and 2.5 million children were living with HIV in the world (according to estimates from the Joint United Nations Programme on HIV/AIDS (UNAIDS) and the World Health Organization (WHO), reported in *http://www.avert.org/worlstatinfo.htm,* last updated December 9, 2003).

Muslims believe that sex education should give clear warnings, and discourage sexual experimentation before marriage. The advice usually offered to people (especially young people), in the efforts to prevent sexually transmitted diseases (STDs) without 'spoiling sexual enjoyment', frequently overlooks the doubtful advisability and morality of casual sexual liaisons. Instead of assuming that because some people are sexually active at a young age all young people must be given as much information and contraceptive advice as possible, more attention should be paid to getting the message across that 'No sex outside marriage' is the most effective form of protection from sexually transmitted diseases.

The concept of what constitutes 'acceptable' behaviour in society needs to be redefined. It is often said that if you want to know the future, look into the past: history shows that some civilisations collapsed once homosexuality was tolerated as normal behaviour. Sadly, in this secular world, the guidance given by *Allāh* is rejected more often than not. It is shocking for Muslim parents to read that "Only 3 per cent of young people [aged 16 – 24] believe that sexual intercourse should be reserved for marriage, with nearly half admitting to their first experience before the age of 16..." (*The Independent*, 21 July 1992).

A stable, responsible and caring society is only possible where sexual relationships are based on heterosexual marriage; there should be no place for extramarital affairs and deviant practices such as homosexuality.

Premarital relationships and Islām

To many the fact that such an issue is even discussed in this book is strange; after all, having a boyfriend or a gilrfriend is seen as being normal and anyone not having had such a relationship is deemed to be either abnormal or severely dysfunctional.

There are certain urges and desires which are basic to human nature, one of these is the desire to share intimate love with a member of the opposite sex. This need not necessarily be motivated by simple sexual urge, although it may play a major role. Islām, contrary to popular opinion, does not refuse to recognize such desires, rather it shows a way of fulfilling such desires for both the greater good of the individual and society. This way is that of marriage. An ideal Islāmic marriage allows the partners to develop greater love, comfort and pleasure between husband and wife through seeking the pleasure of Allāh.

Unfortunately we live in a world where the ideal very rarely exists in the reality. In Western societies today, women and men are often simply encouraged to do what is 'natural', ignoring ethical and moral considerations arising out of such actions. Present day issues which are considered societal norms would have been frowned upon as serious breaches of morality, and detrimental to the welfare of society only a generation ago.

Islāmic society is governed by its sense of collective and individual responsibility to Allāh Who clearly alone has the right to define human limits of behaviour. In the light of that Governance the family is rightfully considered the foremost institution of society and accordingly measures are taken to honour and safeguard its purity and integrity. Amongst such measures is the prevention of treating women as mere 'sex objects', used at will without the commitment of a stable relationship provided for by marriage. Without the bond of marriage there will be children born out of illicit relationships, an increase in one-parent families, teenage and unwanted pregnancies, transmission of sexually transmitted diseases, severe emotional and psychological difficulties, all of which would result in catastrophic consequences for the society in which we live.

Muslims believe that Allāh does not forbid or allow certain behaviour, except that such measures relate to our best interests, guiding us away from potentially destructive behavior and towards behavior that allows us to achieve our most fulfilling potentials as human beings.

The Qur'ān says:

> ***"Tell the believing men to lower their gaze***
> ***and guard their private parts.***
> ***That is purer for them. Surely Allāh knows what they do.***
> ***And tell the believing women to lower their gaze***
> ***and guard their private parts..."***
>
> ***{Al-Qur'ān, chapter 24, verse 30–31}***

This Qur'ānic directive is not to develop a society where people spend most of the time looking down at the floor, rather it seeks to develop a strong sense of reserve, modesty and mutual respect in the presence of the opposite sex. Thus a conscious Muslim man or woman should seek to avoid anything which may lead him or her towards indecency, including dressing in a certain way, avoiding certain places, and in some cases avoiding certain people.

So to summarize, Islām does not seek to undermine that flutter of the heart, those emotions called love that one may feel, feelings brought on by our hormones and our basic nature as human beings. Keeping people apart in total separation does not necessarily make a difference to these urges and feelings, in fact to deny them would be to deceive oneself. Islām states that such feelings are a Sign from Allāh and should be cherished and maintained in a stable, lasting relationship, a commitment that in an increasingly unstable and materialistic world can only be truly fulfilled through marriage.

> ***And among His signs is this,***
> ***that He created for you mates from among yourselves,***
> ***that you may dwell in tranquillity with them***
> ***and He has put love and mercy between your hearts.***
> ***Verily in that are signs for those who reflect.***
> ***{Al-Qur'ān, chapter 30, verse 21}***

Contraception

Sex education invariably includes a study of contraceptive devices and methods to prevent conception or pregnancy. Contraception is seen by some as being the best way to allow young people to experiment with sexuality without the fear of unwanted pregnancy. Although contraception is often called 'planned parenthood', the way this has been imposed at the behest of the International Monetary Fund (IMF), the World Bank and the United Nations Educational, Scientific and Cultural Organisation (UNESCO) may be called 'forced population control' mainly for economic and political reasons. Such policy is in conflict with a basic Islamic human right and it is the consensus of Muslim scholars that no population control policy should be applied on people.

In a society where extramarital and premarital sex are forbidden and there is no free-mixing between adult men and women, contraception as the means to prevent pregnancy becomes less necessary. However, the fact that contraception unlike abortion does not involve the killing of an already existing foetus has led to a great majority of Muslim jurists having tolerant views towards it.

Imām Ghazālī (1058–1111) drew a clear distinction between contraception and abortion: "Contraception is not like abortion. Abortion is a crime against an existing being. Existence has various stages. The first is the settling of the semen in the womb and its mixing with the secretions [egg] of the woman. It is then ready to receive life. Disturbing it is a crime. When it develops further and becomes a lump, abortion is a greater crime. When it acquires a soul and its creation is complete the crime becomes even more grievous. The crime reaches its maximum seriousness after the foetus is separated from its mother alive." (*Al-Iḥyā'*, book of *An-Nikāḥ* [Marriage], p.74). Ghazālī wrote about the permissibility of contraception and enumerated a wide range of conditions under which it could be practised, these generally included health hazards and specific socio-economic factors although such contraception is highly discouraged.

As for those who fear they would not be able to provide for the child should they become pregnant, they may take heart by considering *Allāh's* promise in the *Qur'ān*:

... No soul shall have a burden laid on it
greater than it can bear.
No mother shall be treated unfairly on account of her child.
Nor father on account of his child.
{Al-Qur'ān, chapter 2, verse 233}

In specific cases where contraception is allowed in Islam, mutual consent is a condition.

"A man must not practise withdrawal ('Azl) with his wife unless she freely consents."

{Ibn Mājah, Ḥadīth 1918. www.al-islam.com (Arabic)}

It is interesting to note that outcries about shortage of resources in the face of population growth conveniently sidetrack complementary solutions such as the redistribution of wealth on both a national and international level, the reduction in military expenditure and an allocation of more resources towards humantitarian causes.

It should be borne in mind that contraception is not always reliable or safe, either in preventing pregnancy or the transmission of diseases (STDs). Condoms, which could be loosely equated with *coitus interruptus* (*'Azl*), do not give 100% protection. Some Muslim jurists allow *coitus interruptus* on the basis of some of the sayings of Prophet Muḥammad ﷺ. The 'Pill' has recently been linked to harmful side effects, such as an increased risk of breast cancer. It is the intention which is important in making a decision about contraception. Practising Muslims will always put their total trust in *Allāh* and live a decent life, trying their best to emulate the *Sunnah* of the Prophet ﷺ. We must remember that no human being has the power to stop what *Allāh* wills to happen. Regarding the practice of coitus interruptus, the Prophet ﷺ remarked:

"If you wish so you may. And if Allah willed for her something (pregnancy), she will have it."
{Muslim Vol. 2, Ḥadīth 3383, p. 734}

Abortion

While Islām for certain valid reasons does allow for the prevention of pregnancy through means such as contraception, Muslim jurists unanimously agree that once a foetus is completely formed and deemed alive, aborting it is strongly prohibited (Ḥarām). This is because abortion in such cases constitutes an offence against a living human being and human life in Islam is sacrosanct.

> ***Do not take life –***
> ***which Allāh has made sacred –***
> ***except for just cause.***
> ***{Al-Qur'ān, chapter 17, verse 33}***

> ***On that account We ordained for the Children of Israel***
> ***that if any one slew a person –***
> ***unless it be for murder or for spreading mischief in the land –***
> ***it would be as if he slew the whole people.***
> ***And if any one saved a life***
> ***it would be as if he saved the life of the whole people.***
> ***{Al-Qur'ān, chapter 5, verse 32}***

> ***We have honoured the sons of Ādam…***
> ***{Al-Qur'ān, chapter 17, verse 70}***

There is scholarly debate amongst Muslims about the exact point a human foetus could be deemed to have life; this is because of differences of interpretation of a prophetic saying regarding the time at which the soul enters the human body (See: Al-Bukhārī Vol. 9 p.411. See also Zarabozo's commentary on Fourty Ḥadīth, Ḥadīth No. 4, Vol. 1, p.387 onwards, and. p.408 onwards). Some scholars state the process to begin 40 days after conception while others say it is 120. In either case, abortion is prohibited except under exceptional circumstances, which may include: rape, foetal deformity of the type of anencephaly (no brain), congenital rubella, specific mental, physical complications for the mother.

The Human Fertilisation and Embryology Act 1990 allows abortion on the following conditions (See section 37: Amendment of law relating to termination of pregnancy):

1) That the pregnancy has not exceeded its twenty-fourth week and that the

continuance of the pregnancy would involve risk, greater than if the pregnancy were terminated, of injury to the physical or mental health of the pregnant woman or any existing children of the family; or

2) That the termination is necessary to prevent grave permanent injury to the physical or mental health of the pregnant woman; or

3) That the continuance of the pregnancy would involve risk to the life of the pregnant woman greater than if the pregnancy were terminated; or

4) That there is a substantial risk that if the child were born it would suffer from such physical or mental abnormalities as to be seriously handicapped.

It should also be noted that although UK law (The Human Fertilisation and Embryology Act 1990) allows abortion as long as the foetus has not exceeded its twenty-fourth week, premature babies at 20 -23 weeks have demonstrated survival within hospitals in this country. The Law is not applied as it should be. It is widely accepted that in practice, women in the UK get abortion on demand.

In the modern world where ultrasound scanners can detect from the sixth week whether the foetus is male or female, babies are becoming increasingly vulnerable in certain parts of the world where abortions may be carried out simply because the child is female. In some regions such infanticide is seriously affecting the balance of the population.

In Arabia before the advent of Islām the tribal custom was to bury unwanted baby girls alive. This abominable practice was totally prohibited and there are two verses of the Qur'ān connected with that which could also be applied directly to the circumstances of abortion:

> ***Slay not your children, fearing a fall to poverty,***
> ***We shall provide for them and for you.***
> ***Lo! the slaying of them is a great sin***
> ***{Al-Qur'ān, chapter 17, verse 31}***

> ***When the female (infant), buried alive, is questioned –***
> ***For what crime was she killed?***
> ***{Al-Qur'ān, chapter 81, verses 8–9}***

Those who advocate the belief that abortion is permissible because 'a woman has the right to decide what she does with her own body' should remember that it is *not* just 'her own body' but also the body of another; as the mother of an unborn child, there is a separate but totally dependent living human being inside her created by the Will of *Allāh*, entitled to her utmost care and protection. If, for any reason, the mother fears the pregnancy is too much to bear, then it is up to the family, the community and society at large to give her every support and comfort. But that child's life must not be deliberately ended.

If, however, it is reliably established that the continuation of the pregnancy will result in the death of the mother, then the principle of choosing the lesser of two evils is followed, and an abortion is allowable. The mother's life takes precedence over that of her baby in such an instance because the mother is already established in life with many duties and responsibilities. It is thus less disruptive to family life (although just as regrettable) to sacrifice the life of the unborn child which has not yet acquired a personality nor has any duties, responsibilities or obligations. Abortion is also linked to the increased risk of Breast Cancer.

The widespread availability of abortion has meant the slaughter of millions of unborn children. Recent statistics released by the Goverment pertaining to legal abortions carried out under the 1967 Abortion Act in 2002 show over 175, 500 abortions taking place within England and Wales with over 3,500 of them consisting of girls aged 15 and under (See: Office of National Statistics, Abortion Statistics, England and Wales: 2002, Tables 1 and 2). This staggering figure does not include abortions carried out by non-residents and the large number of underground abortions carried out on the basis of perceived 'physical deformities'. The murder of these tiny human beings could have been avoided by behaving correctly and obeying *Allāh's* laws.

Sex and Relationships Education (SRE) in Schools

Allāh has made natural arrangements for humans to learn about their sexuality as they grow and develop but young people are in need of knowledge and understanding to cope with real-life situations. Hence, as mentioned earlier the subject of sex was not a taboo amongst early Muslim scholars and they gave specific information and guidance on reproduction, menstruation, childbirth and marriage. There are also clear guidelines on sexual etiquette within marriage. Any sexual activity outside marriage is clearly forbidden.

> ***O Mankind! If you have a doubt about the Resurrection,***
> ***(consider) that We created you out of dust, then out of sperm,***
> ***then out of a leech-like clot*** [***'alaqah***],
> ***then out of a morsel of flesh,***
> ***partly formed and partly unformed...***
> ***{Al-Qur'ān, chapter 22, verse 5}***

> ***Proclaim! (or read!)***
> ***in the name of thy Lord and Cherisher, Who created –***
> ***Created man out of a (mere) leech-like clot*** [***'alaq***].
> ***{Al-Qur'ān, chapter 96, verses 1–2}***

Since there may be many sceptics who doubt the validity of using the Qur'ānic text as a teaching aid in SRE it may be worthwhile to know that the word *'alaq*, which is translated in the above verses as 'a leech-like clot', contains within it the meaning that this is 'something which clings'. It is now known, after 1400 years of the revelation of the *Qur'ān*, that the fertilised egg literally *clings* to the wall of the mother's womb!

Although parents usually find it difficult to talk about sex with their children (and surveys have shown that parents shy away from this), they are in most cases the right people to deal with this delicate and important topic. The law of England and Wales places sex education on the curriculum in every maintained secondary school under section 2 of the Education Reform Act 1988 (as amended by section 241(1) of the Education Act 1993), and at the discretion of school governors in all maintained primary schools under section 18(2) of the Education (No 2) Act 1986.

Muslims must look for ways to ensure their children receive responsible sex education based on the values of family life and morality. Both Muslim and non-Muslim parents should work towards a sex education programme that promotes sexual relations only within the framework of marriage, emphasizing the value of family life, morality and decency, focussing on the dangers of extramarital sexual relationships devoid of any responsibility and accountability. Within an Islāmic context such values and code of coduct do not change with time and place. Muslims must work towards the full recognition of their religious needs by those in authority, when in a non-Muslim country or environment.

A responsible, happy and contented society should be the aim of all, rather than a society that struggles with problems resulting from unbridled liberal and permissive sexual behaviour.

The content of Sex and Relationships Education

In Islām, marriage is the only basis for family life and sexual relationships, in contrast to the society in which we live, where extramarital sex is not only tolerated but has become the norm. Muslims, therefore, should urge schools to make sure the sex education they provide is given '...with due regard to moral considerations and the value of family life.' [Education (No 2) Act 1986, *Section 46*]

Sex and Relationships Education (SRE), is about learning about sex, sexuality, feelings, relationships, sex-related disease, abortion, contraception and physical aspects of reproduction (as a part of the National Science Curriculum).

"Moral considerations and the value of family life" do form part of SRE but the inclusion of 'relationships' outside marriage has undermined the importance of marriage and family life. The legislative proposal outlined in the Queen's Speech on 27 November 2003 allowing registration of civil partnerships between same sex couples will undermine the importance of marriage and family life even further.

All schools must prepare a separate written statement of their policy with regard to the provision of SRE, and must make copies available free of charge to parents of any child registered at the school if they ask for one [*Education*

Act 1993, section 241(5)]. Further, schools must publish in their prospectus a summary of the content and organisation of any sex education they provide [*Education (Schools Information) Regulations 1993; sec 371 (3 a–b), Education Act, 1996*]

The DfEE (Department for Education and Employment) Circular 0116/2000 – *Sex and Relationship Education Guidance, which replaced Circular 5/94 Education Act 1993: Sex Education in schools,* gives important advice about what is expected of school sex education. Muslim, and indeed many non-Muslim, parents would note that it addresses some of their concerns about this subject. The teaching of sex education and its policies should be developed in such a way that they, *"...reflect the parents' wishes and the community they serve."* [Circular 0116/2000, paragraph 8, page 4]

Circular 0116/2000 says that sex education: "is lifelong learning about physical, moral and emotional development. It is about the understanding of the importance of marriage for family life, *'stable and loving relationships,'* respect, love and care. It is also about the teaching of sex, sexuality, and sexual health. It is not about the promotion of sexual orientation or sexual activity – this would be inappropriate teaching." [emphasis ours] [Circular 0116/2000, paragraph 9, page 5]

Muslim and many non-Muslim parents will be upset to note that under the guise of 'stable and loving relationships' the importance and value of family life has been undermined by this Circular, which was not the case with the Circular 5/94.

This Circular gives specific guidlines on sex education in primary schools. These are:

"The Department recommends that all primary schools should have a sex and relationship education programme tailored to the age and the physical and emotional maturity of the children. It should ensure that both boys and girls know about puberty and how a baby is born – as set out in Key Stages 1 and 2 of the National Science Curriculum. Section 3 gives further information on what should be taught at these stages and how this should be rooted in the PSHE (Personal, social and health education) framework." [Circular 0116/2000, paragraph 1.12, page 9]

"All children, including those who develop earlier than the average, need to know about puberty before they experience the onset of physical changes. In the early primary school years, education about relationships needs to focus on friendship, bullying and the building of self-esteem." [Circular 0116/2000, paragraph 1.13, page 9]

"Meeting these objectives will require a graduated, age-appropriate programme of sex and relationship education. Teaching methods need to take account of the developmental differences of children and the potential for discussion on a one-to-one basis or in small groups. Schools should set a framework for establishing what is appropriate and inappropriate in a whole-class setting. Teachers may require support and training in answering questions that are better not dealt with in front of a whole class." [Circular 0116/2000, paragraph 1.14, page 9]

"It is important that the transition year before moving to secondary schools supports pupils' ongoing emotional and physical development effectively. As well as consulting parents more generally about the school's overall policy, primary schools should consult with parents before the transition year about the detailed content of what will be taught. This process should include offering parents support in talking to their children about sex and relationship education and how to link this with what is being taught in school." [Circular 0116/2000, paragraph 1.15, page 9–10]

"Schools should have clear parameters on what children will be taught in the transition year before moving to secondary school. This should include:

• changes in the body related to puberty, such as periods and voice breaking;

• when these changes are likely to happen and what issues may cause young people anxiety and how they can deal with these; and

• how a baby is conceived and born." [Circular 0116/2000, paragraph 1.16, page 10]

On the use of materials the Circular mentions:

"The teaching of some aspects of sex and relationship education might be of concern to teachers and parents. Sensitive issues should be covered by the school's policy and in consultation with parents. Schools of a particular religious ethos may choose to reflect that in their sex and relationship education policy. Research demonstrates that good, comprehensive sex and relationship education does not make young people more likely to enter into sexual activity. Indeed it can help them learn the reasons for, and the benefits to be gained from, delaying such activity." [Circular 0116/2000, paragraph 1.7, page 8]

"Materials used in schools must be in accordance with the PSHE framework and the law. Inappropriate images should not be used nor should explicit material not directly related to explanation. **Schools should ensure that pupils are protected from teaching and materials which are inappropriate, having regard to the age and cultural background of the pupils concerned**. Governors and head teachers should discuss with parents and take on board concerns raised, both on materials which are offered to schools and on sensitive material to be used in the classroom. The Department of Health will be issuing guidance to Health Authorities to make clear that any materials they develop for use in schools must be in line with this guidance. Schools will also want to ensure that children are protected from accessing unsuitable materials on the Internet. The Department's "Superhighways Safety" information pack outlines ways that schools can make access to the Internet safe and prevent children from accessing unsuitable material." [emphasis ours] [Circular 0116/2000, paragraph 1.8, page 8]

The circular also mentions that the National Healthy School Standard (NHSS) introduced in 1999 includes specific themes on sex education:

"The National Healthy School Standard (NHSS) was introduced in October 1999 to support and complement the new PSHE framework. Sex and relationship education is one of a number of specific themes which make up the Standard. The NHSS has specific criteria which ensure that schools can confidently set the context and ethos for the effective delivery of sex and relationship education." [Circular 0116/2000, paragraph 1.9, page 8–9]

The Circular proposed to set a balance between the focus on physical aspects of reproduction and the discussion about feelings, relationships and values. While doing so, stable and loving relationships outside marriage have been mentioned. Muslims will obviously feel upset by this.

"Young people, when asked about their experiences of sex education at school, often complain about the focus on the physical aspects of reproduction and the lack of any meaningful discussion about feelings, relationships and values. Sex and relationship education set within the framework for PSHE across the four key stages will significantly redress that balance. It will help young people to respect themselves and others, and understand difference. Within the context of talking about relationships, children should be taught about the nature of marriage and its importance for family life and for bringing up children. *The Government recognises that there are strong and mutually supportive relationships outside marriage.* Therefore, children should learn the significance of marriage and stable relationships as key building blocks of community and society. Teaching in this area needs to be sensitive so as not to stigmatise children on the basis of their home circumstances." [emphasis ours][Circular 0116/2000, paragraph 1.21, page 11]

Islām does not support the view of the government that there should be stable and supportive relationships outside marriage. Islām does not recognise any extra-marital relationships.

SRE should provide factual information objectively and educate young people to look forward to adult life with a sense of responsibility, accountabilty, happiness and building a strong, stable family life. Objective discussion based on clear and accurate information on all forms of sexuality could be useful depending on how these discussions are conducted. Muslim parents will be reassured if during SRE the Islāmic viewpoint is properly discussed.

Advice to schools and governors

Schools and their governers should sensitively and objectively consider the Islāmic Perspective on SRE and this should form a part of school Sex education programmes. The role of the Muslim Governers of a school is important in this respect. They should consult Muslim parents and represent their views on discussion about the SRE programme of the school.

Headteachers should consult the Imāms of the local mosques and Muslim organisations when they receive representation from Muslim parents on any aspect of SRE.

Requests from Muslim parents should be dealt with carefully and sensitively using professional expertise and empathy. Some Muslim parents have strong views on aspects of SRE and these should be tactfully and sensitively dealt with.

Circular 0116/2000 on SRE deals with the concerns of parents in sections 5.5 to 5.7 on page 26. These are:

"The role of parents as sex educators is emphasised in the Home Office strategy, "Supporting Families", as is their need for support from professionals. The Teenage Pregnancy report also recommends that parents are given more help to talk to their children about sex and relationships. National and local media campaigns will target parents. Each local authority area has a co-ordinator who will encourage schools to identify and develop effective approaches of supporting parents." [Circular 0116/2000, paragraph 5.5, page 26]

"Schools should always work in partnership with parents, consulting them regularly on the content of sex and relationship education programmes. Reflection around parents' own experiences of sex education can often lead to a productive discussion in which teachers and parents can start planning sex and relationship education provision for their children. Parents need to know that the school's sex and relationship education programme will complement and support their role as parents and that they can be actively involved in the determination of the school's policy." [Circular 0116/2000, paragraph 5.6, page 26]

"Parents have the right to withdraw their children from all or part of the sex and relationship education provided at school except for those parts included in the statutory National Curriculum (see section 3). Schools should make alternative arrangements in such cases. The DfEE will offer schools a standard pack of information for parents who withdraw their children from sex and relationship education." [emphasis ours] [Circular 0116/2000, paragraph 5.7, page 26]

When schools publish details of their SRE programme, they should bear in mind that some parents whose first language is not English may need to have translations of the school's policy. Schools should ensure that parents understand the right of withdrawal and how to exercise it." [*Paragraph 0116/2000*]. If aspects of SRE occur in other areas of the curriculum (excepting those parts in the statutory National Curriculum) parents should be informed. Schools would benefit from an exercise which identifies all those areas of the curriculum where SRE issues may arise. Parents should be made aware of these areas of the curriculum.

It would be wrong and unfair for schools to put any pressure on parents who decide to exercise the right of withdrawal. There have been many instances where teachers or headteachers have put great pressure on parents who wanted to withdraw their children from SRE. The Muslim Educational Trust has dealt with a number of cases where the attitude of the school authorities (headteacher and governors) was less than helpful in solving the legitimate concerns of Muslim parents, many of whom admittedly are not as well acquainted with education laws and not as articulate as the authorities. In our opinion, all such problems are not difficult to solve given understanding, empathy, goodwill and a common concern to help the child grow up responsibly towards adult life in the society in which he/she lives.

Goodwill and understanding are essential if problems are to be resolved in a manner acceptable to all and there should be an amicable way of looking at the problems arising out of sex education. Preconceived ideas and a lack of knowledge producing ill-founded fears on both sides should not be used as excuses for closing the doors of consultation. Long-cherished beliefs and values should be respected and the authorities should deal sensitively and professionally with difficulties faced by Muslims in all aspects of life, including sex education.

Advice to Muslim parents

The basic responsibility for passing faith and heritage to young children rests largely with parents, who should set a good example for their children. If they set a bad example, it makes it harder for those children to discover the true standards of Islām for themselves, and the beauty of being born to a Muslim family may be lost. Young Muslims must deal with a multi-faith, multicultural society and try to carve their own niche outside the home. If parents set them good examples then it is reasonable to hope that they will try to emulate their elders and, in turn, set a good example for their own children in the future.

As we have said, parents should ideally be able to give their children advice on sexual matters in accordance with the teachings of Islām. However, many parents may not feel comfortable doing this. Nevertheless, it is the parental duty to ensure that children receive both correct information and protection from immorality. Many parents, both Muslim and non-Muslim, consider discussion about sex with their children a taboo. It might be possible for parents to arrange with a local mosque or *madrasah* for their children to receive Islāmic instruction on these matters from someone more expert or knowledgeable on the subject. They must also make sure that their children have access to good sources of information, particularly Islāmic sources. A list of such sources has been given in the bibliography on pages 59–61. Muslim parents should keep in mind that *Allāh*, the Creator, has given guidance in the *Qur'ān* on matters like procreation, the reproduction process, menstruation, childbirth and marital relationships. Prophet Muḥammad ﷺ gave many guidelines on human sexuality, so parents should not shy away from discussing these matters with their own children, whose welfare is of utmost importance to them. If parents do shy away from their responsibilities, children may learn the wrong things from peers, from the media, from inappropriate sex education materials, or from sexually explicit magazines, books, videos and internet.

Schools should make the SRE policy available to parents who ask. It is very important that parents make every effort to find out what is taught in their children's school, and what materials are used for this purpose. If there are other Muslim and non-Muslim parents at the school sharing these concerns, they may find it easier to work together. Working with people of other faiths for a common good or truth is in accordance with the prophetic example. SRE may not always be delivered as a separate subject. Where it occurs in the National Curriculum Science Order, which is restricted to purely biological aspects, there is no right of withdrawal. But sex education may arise in other areas, such as, PHSE, English, Drama, Citizenship and so on. Parents should make sure that if this happens, it is with their full knowledge and consent.

Parents (Muslims and non-Muslims) should be aware that some of the material prepared for sex education lessons is produced by outside agencies whose objectives may not be the same as theirs. All the resources to be used by the school should be scrutinised in detail by Muslim parents before they agree to it being given or shown to their children. This includes books, videos, leaflets, work sheets, and any other material to be used. **It is preferable if parents and the school work together to develop a SRE policy that meets both the legal and Islāmic requirements. When this is not possible, which is sometimes the case, parents will then have to exercise the legal right to withdraw their children from the SRE programme, without any fear or duress.**

Parents should make sure that the SRE curriculum follows the advice given in the Circular 0116/2000. Furthermore, the curriculum should warn against aspects of this permissive society, where sex outside of marriage is not considered sinful by many, rather is accepted as a norm. Pupils should be informed that no contraceptive method – *apart from abstinence* – is 100% safe (e.g. they should be told that out of 733 women who had abortions in one British city between September 1988 and March 1989, 334 reported that their partners used condoms for contraceptive 'protection' [Source: *The British Journal of Family Planning*, 1990, 15:112-117]); that there are dangerous side-effects to 'The Pill'; that sexually transmitted diseases are dangerous and that abortion is forbidden except in exceptional circumstances. Details of the emotional effects of early sexual intercourse should also be prominent in SRE.

If children are in a mixed-sex school, parents should ask for single-sex lessons on sex education to be arranged, especially on matters such as contraception, as this will ensure the confident participation of all pupils, something that may not always be forthcoming in mixed-sex classes.

Muslim parents' efforts should be directed towards ensuring that the sex education programme at their children's school is not against the basic teachings of their faith. Ultimately, if the school does not produce an acceptable sex education programme, parents have the right to withdraw their children from all or part of it [*Section 17A of the Education Reform Act 1988 (inserted by section 241(2) of the Education Act 1993)*]. Parents do not have to give reasons for their decision nor do they have to indicate what other arrangements they intend to make for providing sex education for their children. But it is preferable to discuss with the Headteacher of the school and explain the religious reasons for exercising the legal right of withdrawal.

Advice to Muslim organisations

Muslim organisations also have the responsibility to help young Muslims grow towards a healthy Islāmic identity. Combined effort from parents and organisations is essential to achieve the desired educational objectives for the benefit of Muslim children in non-Muslim schools. We must act in a concerted and coordinated way to persuade and impress upon those responsible for the education of our children about our particular religious needs. Given a logical, persuasive and articulate approach, most of the educational concerns could be amicably resolved. Of course, there will be circumstances and situations which would need very careful handling on the part of the authorities and Muslims. However, accommodation and understanding of diverse views are not unattainable. We must work towards this. Individual parents may find it difficult to affect change in their schools. But when local mosques and Muslim organisations work in a concerted way, schools could be persuaded to devise a SRE programme which would be acceptable to Muslim pupils and parents.

It may be difficult for some schools to obtain accurate information about Islām and the needs of Muslim pupils. Whereas organisations like the Muslim Educational Trust and a number of other national organisations could give help on a national level, local mosques and organisations are ideally placed to ensure that schools in their communities respect the religious requirements of their Muslim pupils.

Advice to Muslim pupils

As a Muslim pupil you should remember that you are required by your religion to grow up as a responsible human being (*Khalīfah* – the agent of *Allāh* on earth) in any society where you live. You must not forget that your duty is to learn and educate yourself to carry out your responsibilities in adult life purposefully and efficiently. You must not be carried away by the 'trendy' ideas which eventually may prove disastrous for you. Remember that as an example of behaviour you have the best of mankind in the Prophet Muḥammad ﷺ, who was a 'Mercy to the Worlds'. We should emulate his example for our success in this life and the life after death. The criterion of what is right and wrong is based on what Allāh revealed to Prophet Muhammad ﷺ, which is the Qur'ān and the example of Prophet Muhammad ﷺ. If we follow our own desires we might go astray. Allāh says :

> ***... And who is more astray than he who follows his own likes and dislikes without any guidance from Allāh. Surely Allāh guides not the wrongdoers. {Al-Qur'ān, chapter 28, verse 50}***
>
> ***... perhaps you hate a thing and it is good for you; and perhaps you love a thing and it is bad for you. {Al-Qur'ān, chapter 2, verse 216}***

It is in this context you should know that it is your right to have correct information about sexual matters in accordance with the teachings of Islām. Sex is an integral part of human life and therefore you should not feel shy to ask questions to your parents, whose main concern is your welfare, success and prosperity. However, if it is difficult to discuss the subject with your parents, you should try to find a knowledgeable, practising Muslim who can answer your questions. This may be a local *Imām* or Islāmic Studies teacher, a knowledgeable community leader, or an approachable and knowledgeable relative. You should also try to read reliable books (such as those marked with * in the bibliography on pages 59–61). You can even write to Islāmic organisations for advice and information.

There are many non-Muslim organisations who advise on matters of SRE. Some of these have an attitude to life that does not fit with the beliefs and teachings of Islām. It is important, then, that you treat information from such organisations with care and caution.

The great majority of teachers will have a keen interest in your welfare, and will want to be able to give you advice should you need it. You should make sure that this advice does not in any way go against your beliefs as a Muslim. You should tell your parents if any books, videos or other materials used for sex education are in any way offensive or embarrassing, so that they can be checked to make sure they are not against Islāmic teachings. Never try to hide things from your parents; feel confident to talk to your parents and do not feel embarrassed. Remember, this affects your life and it is very important that you should tell your parents what you are taught as a part of SRE in your schools.

The Internet has its enormous benefits but it is not without dangers. It would be to your benefit and welfare not to be induced to go into unethical and unislāmic sites which would lead to disastrous consequences which have been highlighted in the media. Always remember: our Loving and Merciful Creator knows every aspect of our life, we cannot hide anything from Him. This consciousness of Allāh (Taqwā) is the key to our success in this world and in the Ākhirah.

Homosexual practices are not allowed in Islām; they incur the anger of *Allāh*, and are severely punished in an Islāmic society. Schools should not promote homosexuality. If there are teachers or pupils in your school who are homosexual, that is their business, and you should leave them alone.

Islām does not approve of free mixing between sexes. If you are in a mixed sex school, try to restrict your friendships to your own sex; do not seek to be alone with pupils of the opposite sex. Boyfriend-girlfriend relationships inevitably lead to problems, and mean going against the teachings of Islām. Remember, these teachings are designed for your own benefit and welfare. We pray that you adhere to these teachings and gain success in this life and the Hereafter.

Appendix

Sections of the various Acts relevant to the text:

Education Act 1944

Section 76

... local education authorities shall have regard to the general principle that, so far as is compatible with the provision of efficient instruction and training and the avoidance of unreasonable public expenditure, pupils are to be educated in accordance with the wishes of their parents.

Education (No. 2) Act 1986

Section 17

(1) It shall be the duty of every local education authority—

(*a*) *to determine, and keep under review, their policy in relation to the secular curriculum for the county, voluntary and special schools maintained by them ...*

Section 241(3) of the Education Act 1993 inserts the right of withdrawal at this point.

Section 18

(2) The articles of government for every such school shall provide for it to be the duty of the governing body—

(*a*) *to consider separately ... whether sex education should form part of the secular curriculum for the school*

(*b*) *to make, and keep up to date, a separate written statement—*

(i) of their policy with regard to the content and organisation of the relevant part of the curriculum; or

(ii) where they conclude that sex education should not form part of the secular curriculum, of that conclusion.

(3) The article of government for every such school shall provide for it to be the duty of the governing body—

(a) when considering the matters mentioned ... above, to do so in consultation with the head teacher and to have regard—

(i) to any representations which are made to them with regard to any of those matters, by any persons connected with the community served by the school; ...

Section 241(6) of the Education Act 1993 excludes secondary schools from the terms of Section 18(2) of the Education (No. 2) Act 1986 as shown above. Thus, the choice of having sex education in the curriculum or not as detailed in section 18 applies only to primary schools.

Section 241(5) of the Education Act 1993 extends the requirements of Section 18(2) to grant-maintained schools.

Section 20

The Secretary of State shall make regulations requiring the governing body of every county, voluntary and maintained special school to make available to parents of registered pupils at the school, in such form and manner and at such times as may be prescribed—

(a) such information as to the syllabuses to be followed by those pupils; and

(b) such other information as to the educational provision made for them by the school; as may be prescribed.

Section 46

The local education authority by whom any county, voluntary or special school is maintained, and the governing body and head teacher of the school, shall take such steps as are reasonably practicable to secure that where sex education is given to any registered pupils at the school it is given in such a manner as to encourage those pupils to have due regard to moral considerations and the value of family life.

Education Reform Act 1988

Section 1

(2) The curriculum for a maintained school satisfies the requirements of this section if it is a balanced and broadly based curriculum which—

(a) promotes the spiritual, moral, cultural, mental and physical development of pupils at the school and of society; and

(b) prepares such pupils for the opportunities, responsibilities and experiences of adult life.

Section 2

(1) The curriculum for every maintained school shall comprise a basic curriculum which includes–

(a) provision for religious education for all registered pupils at the school; and

(b) a curriculum for all registered pupils at the school of compulsory school age (to be known as "the National Curriculum") which meets the requirements of subsection (2) below.

Section 23

(1) Every local education authority shall, with the approval of the Secretary of State and after consultation with governing bodies of aided schools and of special agreement schools, make arrangements for the consideration and disposal of any complaint made on or after 1st September 1989 which is to the effect that the authority, or the governing body of any county or voluntary school maintained by the authority or of any special school so maintained which is not established in a hospital—

(a) have acted or are proposing to act unreasonably with respect to the exercise of any power conferred or the performance of any duty imposed on them by or under—

(i) any provision of this Chapter; or

(ii) any other enactment relating to the curriculum for,

religious worship in, maintained schools other than grant-maintained schools; or

(b) *have failed to discharge any such duty.*

Education Act 1993

Section 241

(1) In section 2(1) of the Education Reform Act 1988 (content of curriculum), after "school" in paragraph (a) there is inserted—

"(aa) in the case of a secondary school, provision for sex education for all registered pupils at the school;

(ab) in the case of a special school, provision for sex education for all registered pupils at the school who are provided with secondary education".

(2) In section 114(1) of the Education Act 1944 (interpretation), after the definition of "Senior pupil" there is inserted—

""Sex education" includes education about—

(a) Acquired Immune Deficiency Syndrome and Human Immunodeficiency Virus, and

(b) any other sexually transmitted disease".

(3) After section 17 of the Education Reform Act 1988 there is inserted—

"Exemption from sex education

17A If the parent of any pupil in attendance at any maintained school requests that he may be wholly or partly excused from receiving sex education at the school, the pupil shall, except so far as such education is comprised in the National Curriculum, be so excused accordingly until the request is withdrawn."

(4) The Secretary of State shall so exercise the power conferred by section 4 of that Act to revise the National Curriculum as to secure that the subject of science does not include—

(a) Acquired Immune Deficiency Syndrome and Human Immunodeficiency Virus,

(b) any other sexually transmitted disease, or

(c) aspects of human sexual behaviour, other than biological aspects ...

(5) The governing body of every maintained or grant-maintained school and, in relation to pupils who are provided with secondary education, the governing body of every maintained special school shall—

(a) make, and keep up to date, a separate written statement of their policy with regard to the provision of sex education, and

(b) make copies of the statement available for inspection (at all reasonable times) by parents of registered pupils at the school and provide a copy of the statement free of charge to any such parent who asks for one.

(6) In relation to any county, or controlled, secondary school, and in relation to any pupils who are provided with secondary education in a maintained special school, section 18 of the Education (No. 2) Act 1986 (policy for curriculum in county etc. schools), shall have effect with the omission of subsections (2) and (6)(c)(i) and of references to the matters mentioned in subsection (2) of that section.

Education Act 1996

Section 352. - *(1) The curriculum for every maintained school shall comprise a basic curriculum which includes-*

(c) in the case of a secondary school, provision for sex education for all registered pupils at the school, and

(d) in the case of a special school, provision for sex education for all registered pupils at the school who are provided with secondary education.

Section 371. - *(1) This section applies to the articles of government for a county, controlled or maintained special school.*

(2) The articles shall require the governing body to consider-

(c) *how (if at all) the authority's policy with regard to matters other than sex education should in their opinion be modified in relation to the school, and to make, and keep up to date, a written statement of their conclusions.*

(3) The articles shall require the governing body-

(a) *to consider separately (while having regard to the local education authority's statement under section 370) the question whether sex education should form part of the secular curriculum for the school, and*

(b) *to make, and keep up to date, a separate written statement-*

(i) *of their policy with regard to the content and organisation of the relevant part of the curriculum, or*

(ii) *where they conclude that sex education should not form part of the secular curriculum, of that conclusion.*

Sex education: manner of provision.

Section 403. - *(1) The local education authority, governing body and head teacher shall take such steps as are reasonably practicable to secure that where sex education is given to any registered pupils at a maintained school, it is given in such a manner as to encourage those pupils to have due regard to moral considerations and the value of family life.*

(2) *In subsection (1) "maintained school" includes a maintained special school established in a hospital.*

Sex education: statements of policy.

Section 404. - *(1) The governing body of a maintained school shall-*

(a) *make, and keep up to date, a separate written statement of their policy with regard to the provision*

of sex education, and

(b) *make copies of the statement available for inspection (at all reasonable times) by parents of registered pupils at the school and provide a copy of the statement free of charge to any such parent who asks for one.*

Exemption from sex education.

Section 405. *If the parent of any pupil in attendance at a maintained school requests that he may be wholly or partly excused from receiving sex education at the school, the pupil shall, except so far as such education is comprised in the National Curriculum, be so excused accordingly until the request is withdrawn.*

The Ethical Standards in Public Life Bill, Scotland, 2000

The Scottish Parliament voted to repeal Section 28 of the Local Government Act by 99 votes to 17 on 21st June 2000. The legislation was part of the Ethical Standards in Public Life Bill. Section 28, stated that a local authority is not permitted to "...promote the teaching in any maintained school of the acceptability of homosexuality as a pretended family relationship." The Act did not apply directly to schools but governed Local Authorities.

Learning and Skills Bill 2000

Clause 117 *of the bill updates and amends the Education Act 1996*

Local education authorities no longer have any responsibility for sex education in maintained schools; this now rests with the school's governing body and head teacher. [*(2) and (3)*]

National Science Curriculum.

Sex and Relationship Education (SRE) (Ref: DfES 0706/2001)

Key Stage 1

- *Animals, including humans, move, feed, grow, use their sense and reproduce*
- *Children should recognise and name the main external parts of the human body.*
- *That human can produce offspring and these grow into adults*
- *Children should recognise similarities and differences between themselves and other and treat others with sesitivly*

Key Stage 2

- *Life process common to humans include nutrition, growth and reproduction*
- *The main stages of human lifecystyle.*

Key Stage 3

- *Fertilization in humans is the fusion of a male and female cell*
- *Student should know the physical and emotional changes that take place during adolescence*
- *The human reproductive cycle, including the menstrual cycle and fertilisation*
- *How the growth and reproduction of bacteria and the replication of viruses can effects human health.*

Key Stage 4

- *Hormonal control in humans, including the effects of sex hormones*
- *Medical uses of hormones, including the control and promotion of fertility*
- *How sex is determined in humans.*

[*Sex and relationship education (SRE) (Ref: DfES 0706/2001*]

Sexual Offences (Amendment) Bill, 2001

The Sexual Offences (Amendment) Bill came into effect on January 8th 2001, and reduced the age of sexual consent for gay men from 18 to 16 in England, Wales and Scotland. In Northern Ireland, the age of consent for gay men was brought into line with the heterosexual age of consent at 17.

Local Government Act 1988

Section 28

(1) The following section shall be inserted after section 2 of the Local Government Act 1986 (prohibition of political publicity)—

"Prohibition on promoting homosexuality by teaching or by publishing material

2A.—(1) A local authority shall not—

(a) intentionally promote homosexuality or publish material with the intention of promoting homosexuality;

(b) promote the teaching in any maintained school of the acceptability of homosexuality as a pretended family relationship.

(2) Nothing in subsection (1) above shall be taken to prohibit the doing of anything for the purpose of treating or preventing the spread of disease.

Local Government Act 1988, England and Wales (Amendment) Bill 2003

The repeal of Section 28 of the local Government act was voted for by the House of commons in March 2003 and by the House of Lords in July 2003. It received its Royal Assent on September 18th 2003.

Bibliography

1. *The Noble Qur'ān*: Eng. translation by Dr Muḥammad Taqīuddīn Al-Hilālī and Dr M. Muḥsin Khān. Maktaba Darussalām, Riyādh, 1994.

2. *The Holy Qur'ān: text, translation and commentary*, 'Abdullāh Yusuf 'Alī, Amana Corporation, USA, 1983.

3. *The Glorious Qur'ān*, translation by Muḥammad Marmaduke Pickthall, Taj Co. Ltd., Karachi, Pakistan, 1975.

4. *Towards Understanding the Qur'ān* (Vol. I–VII), Abul A'lā Mawdūdī, Tafsīr in Urdu, English trans. by Zafar I. Anṣārī, Islāmic Foundation, Leicester, 2001.

5*. *Ṣaḥīḥ Al-Bukhārī* (vols. I – IX), English translation by Dr M. Muḥsin Khan, Dar Al-Arabia, Lebanon, 1985.

6. *Ṣaḥīḥ Muslim* (vols. I–IV), English translation by 'Abdul Ḥamīd Ṣiddiqui, Dar Al-Arabia, Lebanon, 1972

7. *Al-Muwaṭṭa' of Imām Mālik*, English translation by A. A. Tarjumana & Yaqub Johnson, Diwan Press, 1982.

8. *Nailul Awtār* (Arabic, vols. V & VI), Muḥammad bin 'Alī Ibn Muḥammad Ash-Shawkānī, Dar Al-Jīl, Beirut, 1973.

9. *Zādul Ma'ād* (Arabic, vol. V), Ibnul Qayyim, Muassasat Ar-Risālah, Beirut, 1979.

10*. *Fiqhus Sunnah* (Arabic, vols. I), As-Sayyid Sābiq, Dārul Kitāb Al-'Arabi, Beirut, 1977.

11. *Commentary on the Forty Ḥadīth of Al-Nawawī, Jamaal al-Din M. Zarabozo, Boulder, USA, 1999.*

12. *Tarbiyatul 'Awlād Fil Islām* (Arabic, vol. I), Abdullāh Nasiḥ 'Ulwān, Darussalām, Beirut, 1981.

13. *The Qur'ān: Basic Teachings*, Irving, Aḥmad and Aḥsan, The Islāmic Foundation, Leicester, UK, 1979.

14*.*The Lawful and the Prohibited in Islām*, Yusuf Al-Qaraḍāwī, American Trust Publications, USA.

15. *The Laws of Marriage and Divorce in Islām*, Abul A'lā Mawdūdī, translated by Prof Fazl Aḥmad, Islāmic Book Publishers, Kuwait, 1993.

16. *Abortion, Birth Control & Surrogate Parenting – An Islāmic Perspective*, Abul Faḍl Moḥsin Ebrāhim, American Trust Publications, Indianapolis, USA, 1989.

17*. *The Miracle of Life*, Faṭima M. D'Oyen, The Islamic Foundation, Leicester, UK, 1996.

18. *The Muslim Marriage Guide*, Ruqaiyyah Waris Maqsood, Quillam Press, London, UK, 1995.

19. *Gender Equity in Islām*, Jamal Badawī, American Trust Publications, Indiana, USA, 1995.

20. *The Family Structure in Islām*, Ḥammūdah 'Abd al 'Āṭī, American Trust Publications, Indiana, USA, 1977.

21. *Shari'ah: The Islāmic Law*, 'Abdur Raḥmān I. Doi, Ta Ha Publishers, London, UK, 1984.

22. *Ideal Woman in Islām*, Moḥammad 'Imrān, Islamic Publications Ltd, Lahore, Pakistan, 1981.

23. *Sexuality in Islām*, 'Abdul Wahāb Bouhdiba, Routledge & Keegan Paul, 1985.

24. *Sex and Sexuality in Islām: Birth Control before the nineteenth century,* B. F. Musallam, Cambridge, 1983

25. *Some Notes on Sex Education*, London County Council, 1964.

26. *Sex Education: Its Uses and Abuses*, K. H. Kavanah, The Responsible Society, Milton Keynes.

27. *Birth Control: Its Social, Political, Economic, Moral and Religious Aspects*, Abul 'Alā Mawdūdī, Islamic Publications, Lahore, 1974.

28. *Woman in Islām*, Ayesha B. Lemu and Fāṭima Heren, Islamic Foundation, Leicester, UK, 1976.

29. *Woman and Family Life in Islām*, World Assembly of Muslim Youth (WAMY), Riyadh, Saudi Arabia, 1995.

30*. *Hijāb (veil): The View from the Inside*, Kanla Nakata (Japan), Ruth Anderson (USA), World Assembly of Muslim Youth (WAMY), Riyadh, Saudi Arabia, 1995.

31*. *The Muslim Woman's Handbook*, Hudā Khaṭṭāb, Ta Ha Publishers, London, UK, 1993.

32. *Women, Muslim Society and Islām*, Lamyā al-Farūqī, American Trust Publications, Indiana, USA, 1988.

33. *Living with Teenagers (A Guide for Muslim Parents)*, Ruqaiyyah Waris Maqsood, Ta Ha Publishers, London, UK, 1995.

34*. *Muslim Teenagers Coping*, Ruqaiyyah Waris Maqsood, Ta Ha Publishers, London, UK, 2003.

35. *School Sex Education: Why, What and How?*, Doreen E. Massey, Family Planning Association, 1988.

36. *Sex Education: An Islamic Perspective*, Shahīd Aṭhar , M.D, Kazi Publications, 1995.

37. *Islāmic Marriage*. Hedaya Hartford , Dar Al Fikr, Damascus, Syria. 2000.

Digital Sources:

38. *Obstetrics and Gynaecology*. Prof. Ḥassan Ḥathout , Islam Set. <http://www.islamset.com/bioethics/obstet/contobs.html>

39. *What everyone should know about Islām and Muslims*. Suzanne Ḥaneef, Kazi Publications, 1995.

40. *Islām Beliefs and Teachings*, Ghulam Sarwar, The Muslim Educational Trust, 2003.

41. *Thinking about abortion*. Ruqaiyyah Waris Maqsood. <http://www.members.aol.com/ruqaiyyah/articles/abortion.htm>

42. *Why can't we be (Ḥalāl) friends?* Ruqaiyyah Waris Maqsood. <http://www.members.aol.com/ruqaiyyah/articles/halalfriends.htm>.

43. *Arabic Ḥadīth Database* from <www.al-islam.com>.

44. *The Ḥadīth Software*, Version 1.0 2000–2002. (Islamsoft Solutions)

45. *MacḤadīth (Al Ḥadīth)*, Islamic Computing Centre, London UK.

Transliteration

Correct pronunciation of Arabic words is very important. Incorrect pronunciation changes the meaning of an Arabic word. Transliteration marks are shown below as a guide to correct pronunciation. These marks help to show how the words should sound, but it is not possible to show on a printed page exactly how to pronounce words.
For example, the word *Allāh* should be pronounced correctly with the two *Ls* sounded distinctly, and the last *A* has to be a long sound. The name *Muóammad* should be pronounced with a glottal sound of *H* rather than the normal *H* sound, with the two *Ms* sounded clearly.
I have used phonetic transliteration for the benefit of younger learners, e.g. *Sūratul Fātióah* rather than *Sūrah al-Fātióah*, *at-Tashahhud* rather than *al-Tashahhud*, etc.
Ideally, it is best to listen to an Arabic-speaking person, or someone who has learned how to say Arabic words correctly. Audio and video resources can be immensely helpful.

Arabic symbol	Transliteration symbol	English sound	Example	Arabic symbol	Transliteration symbol	English sound	Example
ا	a	add	*Akbar*	ف	f	far	*Fāṭimah*
ب	b	bit	*Bilāl*	ق	q	–	*Qur'ān*
ت	t	tap	*Tirmidhī*	ك	k	king	*Ka'bah*
ث	th	think	*'Uthmān*	ل	l	list	*Luqmān*
ج	j	just	*Jannah*	م	m	mist	*Mūsā*
ح	ó	–	*Muóammad*	ن	n	name	*Nūó*
خ	kh	loch	*Khalīfah*	و	w	wait	*Wụū'*
د	d	dawn	*Dāwūd*	هاه	h	rehash	*Ibrāhīm*
ذ	dh	worthy	*Tirmidhī*	ي	y	year	*Yāsīn*
ر	r	rip	*Raómān*	ة	t *if followed*, h *otherwise*		*Ṣalāh*
ز	z	zip	*Zakāh*	ء	'	–	*Qur'ān*
س	s	sat	*Sunnah*	بَا *(fatha)*	a	tap	*Rajab*
ش	sh	shape	*Shahādah*	بَا	ā	Saab	*Dāwūd*
ص	ṣ	–	*Ṣawm*	بِا *(kasra)*	i	grin	*Jinn*
ض	˛	–	*Ramạān*	بِي	ī	deed	*Khadījah*
ط	ṭ	–	*Ṭahārah*	بُا *(amma)*	u	pull	*Jumu'ah*
ظ	û	–	*Ẓuhr*	بُو	ū	food	*Dāwūd*
ع	'	–	*'Aṣr*	بَو	aw	how	*Ṣawm*
غ	gh	–	*Maghrib*	بَي	ai	tie	*Sulaimān*

Glossary

ﷺ	Arabic written after the name of the Prophet ﷺ, meaning 'peace and blessings of *Allāh* be upon him'.
Abū Dāwūd	One of the noted compilers of *Aḥādīth*, whose main collection is called *Sunan Abū Dāwūd* (d. 888 CE).
Ādam	First human being and first prophet of *Allāh*.
Aḥādīth	(Plural of *Ḥadīth*) Reports of the sayings, deeds and actions approved by Prophet Muḥammad ﷺ.
AIDS	Acquired Immune Deficiency Syndrome.
'Ā'ishah	One of the wives of the Prophet ﷺ, and a noted authority on his *Aḥādīth* (d. 678 CE).
Ākhirah	Life after death. It includes the Day of Judgement and the never-ending life after death.
'Alaq	Word used in the first verses revealed of the *Qur'ān*, usually translated as 'clot'.
Al-Bukhārī	One of the noted compilers of *Aḥādīth*, whose main collection is called *Ṣaḥiḥ Al-Bukhārī* (d. 870 CE).
Al-Qur'ān	This is the sacred book of Muslims, the final book of guidance from *Allāh*, sent down to Muḥammad ﷺ through the angel *Jibrā'īl* (Gabriel) over a period of 23 years.
An-Nasā'ī	One of the noted compilers of *Aḥādīth*, whose main collection is called *Sunan An-Nasā'ī* (d. 915 CE).
At-Tirmidhī	One of the noted compilers of *Aḥādīth*, whose main collection is called *Jāmi' At-Tirmidhī* (d. 892 CE).
'Awrah	Those parts of the body that need to be covered and should not be seen by *Ghair Maḥram*.
'Azl	*Coitus interruptus.*
Bukhārī	(See *Al-Bukhārī*).

DfES	Department for Education and Skills (replaced Department for Education and Employment.DfEE).
Du'ā'	A supplication to *Allāh.*
ERA	Education Reform Act 1988.
Ghair Maḥram	Those relatives who are not part of the *Maḥram.*
Ghazālī	(See *Imām Ghazālī*).
Ghusl	Washing the whole body for *Ṭahārah* when in *Junub.*
Ḥadd	(See *Ḥudūd*).
Ḥadīth	(See *Aḥādīth*).
Ḥayā'	Natural modesty, or the sense of natural shame in a human being, especially in covering the *'awrah.*
HIV	Human Immunodeficiency Virus – the virus that can lead to AIDS.
Ḥudūd	Punishments prescribed in Islāmic law.
Ibn Mājah	One of the noted compilers of *Aḥādīth*, whose main collection is called *Sunan Ibn Mājah* (d. 886 CE).
Imām Ghazālī	Noted scholar of Islām (d. 1111 CE).
Imām Mālik	One of the noted compilers of *Aḥādīth*, whose main collection is called *Al-Muwaṭṭa* (d. 795 CE).
IMF	International Monetary Fund.
Janābah	A state of impurity after sexual intercourse.
Jinn	*Allāh's* creatures created from smokeless fire with free will.
Junub	A person's state after sexual intercourse, wet dreams, menstruation or post-childbirth bleeding.
Khalīfah	Vicegerent of *Allāh* on the earth.
Khamr	Intoxicants, especially alcoholic drink and recreational drugs.
Lot	(See *Lūṭ*).

Lūṭ	Prophet of *Allāh* who warned his people of the evil of their practising homosexuality.
Madrasah	Islāmic school.
Mahr	Dowry or Marital gift, given by the husband to the wife.
Maḥram	Those relatives to whom marriage is prohibited according to Islāmic law.
Mālik	(See *Imām Mālik*).
Muḥammad ﷺ	The final messenger of *Allāh* to mankind (d. 632 CE).
Muslim	A person who freely and consciously accepts the Islāmic way of life, and sincerely practices it. Also, name of one of the noted compilers of *Aḥādīth*, whose main collection is called *Ṣaḥiḥ Muslim*.
Nasā'ī	(See *An-Nasā'ī*).
NHSS	National Healthy Schools Standards
Qadhf	False accusation.
QCA	Qualifications and Curriculum Authority
Qur'ān	(See *Al-Qur'ān*).
SACRE	Standing Advisory Council on Religious Education.
Ṣadaqah	Charitable gift or act.
SCAA	School Curriculum and Assessment Authority (now called QCA).
Shaiṭān	Satan – the devil.
SRE	*Sex and Relationships Education*
STD	Sexually Transmitted Disease.
Sunnah	The example set by Prophet Muḥammad ﷺ, as recorded in *Aḥādīth*.
Ṭahārah	Cleanliness or purification.

Taqwā	Piety – obedience to all *Allāh's* commands.
Tayammum	Dry ablution, performed without water.
Tirmidhī	(See *At-Tirmidhī*).
UNESCO	United Nations Educational, Scientific and Cultural Organisation.
WHO	World Health Organisation.
Wuɖū'	Washing for prayer in prescribed manner.
Zinā	Fornication, adultery.

Index

Muslim Educational Trust publications

1. ***Islām Beliefs & Teachings*** **£6.25**
   by Ghulam Sarwar
   7th edition, 2003, pp240

2. ***Islām for Younger People*** **£3.00**
   by Ghulam Sarwar
   4th edition, 2003, pp64 (new design)

3. ***The Beginner's Book of Ṣalāh*** **£3.00**
   by Ghulam Sarwar
   6th edition, 2003, pp64

4. ***Sex Education – The Muslim Perspective*** **£3.75**
   by Ghulam Sarwar
   4th edition, 2004, pp72

5. ***What does Islām say?*** **£3.75**
   by Ibrahim B. Hewitt
   4th edition, 2004, pp64

6. ***Islāmic Education: its meanings, problems & prospects***
   1st edition, 2001, pp56 **£2.50**

7. ***British Muslims & Schools*** **£2.50**
   by Ghulam Sarwar
   2nd edition, 1994, pp52

Plus a selection of full-colour posters. A catalogue is available on request.

Prices include p&p

Please send your orders, with payment, to:

The Muslim Educational Trust

130 Stroud Green Road, London N4 3RZ

Tel: 020 7272 8502 Fax: 020 7281 3457

www.muslim-ed-trust.org.uk
email:info@muslim-ed-trust.org.uk